FeelGoodGrammar: How to Make Sentences in Business English

Como Escribir Frases En Un Ingles Comercial

商業英語造句新法:說和寫

Yury Lee

For book orders, email orders@traffordpublishing.com.sg

Most Trafford Singapore titles are also available at major online book retailers.

Printed in Singapore.

ISBN: 978-1-4669-3459-7 (sc)
ISBN: 978-1-4669-3460-3 (hc)
ISBN: 978-1-4669-3461-0 (e)

Trafford rev. 02/04/2013

 www.traffordpublishing.com.sg

Singapore
toll-free: 800 101 2656 (Singapore)
Fax: 800 101 2656 (Singapore)

Contents

Introduction...ix

Chapter 1: The Verbs: The Center of the Universe 3

Chapter 2: Two Types of Sentences ONLY (1): Baby Verbs 21

Chapter 3: Two Types of Sentences ONLY (2):
           Non-Baby Verbs...39

Chapter 4: Big Verbs & Small Verbs...59

Chapter 5: Time for Business (Main Tenses)...........................81

Postscript...101

Picture Sources 103

References 107

Preview of Book 2..109

Contents in Detail

Chapter 1: **The *Verb*: The *Center* of the Universe**

- What is a sentence?
- *So if verbs are so big, how do we locate them?*
- So if verbs are so big, how many verbs are there?
- *Making Sentences*
- Key points

Chapter 2: **Two Types of Sentences *ONLY* (1): *Baby Verbs***

- Two types of sentences only?
- *Babies or Non-Babies*
- Making sentences with Baby Verbs (Taking a nap)
- *Making questions with Baby Verbs*
- Key points

Chapter 3: **Two Types of Sentences *ONLY* (2): *Non-Baby Verbs***

- How many Non-Baby Verbs are there?
- *Making sentences with Non-Baby Verbs*
- Making questions with Non-Baby Verbs
- *Key points*

Chapter 4: **Big Verbs & Small Verbs**

- What's wrong with two verbs coming together?
- *What are Big Verbs & Small Verbs?*
- Making sentences
- *Key points*

Chapter 5: *Time* for Business English (*Main Tenses*)

- Four kinds of futures
- *Two types of past*
- Two types of conditions (if)
- *Key points*

Introduction

Why another book on grammar? You probably have been learning quite a lot of grammar, but you are still not clear about how to make a sentence. Why? Is there anything wrong with your approach to learning? If we offer you a funny way, a non-traditional method, a 'new' perspective on thinking about grammar, will you try it?

The aim of this book is to introduce a 'new' perspective on learning grammar, especially for Business English. We start and end with sentences, the most important part in writing, and sometimes speaking. Unlike traditional grammar books that discuss nouns, verbs, adjectives, we go straight to sentences as we believe at the end of the day what you want are actually sentences.

There have been lots of grammar books on sentences. People call them syntax. Yet books on syntax are extremely abstract (difficult) that it is hard for everyone to understand. This book is different, totally. As the name of the book indicates, it makes you feel good about grammar.

How? This book has four features:

- ○ **Focusing on how to make sentences**
  - ■ Most grammar books helps you understand grammar terms.
  - ■ But, we show you how to put them into practice, how to make sentences (written and spoken).

- **Explaining grammar in an *easy, funny* way**
  - For example, to learn *sentence patterns* in English, you'll have to *solve* a *problem* between two women who have to '*share*' a *husband*.
  - For example, to get the differences between the *past simple* and the *present perfect simple*, you'll read a *love story*.
  - You'll also learn funny *names* such as *Lonely, Friendly, Slim,* and *Fat* Verbs.

- **Reading it like *changing TV channels***
  - You can read the book *chapter by chapter,* or
  - You can just *jump* to *whichever* chapter (channel) that *interests you.*

- ***Avoiding* using *jargon***
  - There is *a minimum use of* grammar terms.
  - You'll find terms such as *Baby Verbs* (not the verb 'be'), *Small Verbs* (not gerunds or infinitives).

So, let's *start your journey* of easy grammar, grammar that makes you *feel good,* grammar that teaches you *how to make sentences.*

(*Some of the*) Sentences to Make

Situation	Aim	Sample Sentence
Negotiating	To ask for a *pay rise*	I (really) *feel* that it's about time (for me) to have a pay rise.
At a meeting	To *stop* Mr Trouble *from interrupting you*	I'll *thank* you not to interrupt me *again*.
Talking to coworkers	Use 'thank': a. to *blame* somebody b. to *play tricks on* your teammates who are lazy	We can *thank* Mr Trouble for the trouble (he made). Our team did it, but *no thanks* to you.

D o you want to *speed up* your English learning? If you have a higher level of language proficiency will it make much difference to your *career*?

But *how* are you going to do it? Do you start with nouns, adjectives, adverbs, or infinitives, terms that make you think there is a long way to go? Or is there another way, another approach that *makes grammar easier, makes your life better,* and *makes you feel* good about yourself?

Yes, there is! You can take your *new* way by *starting with sentences,* the big idea behind this '*new*' book on grammar of business English. To start, you have to *throw away all* the *traditional* (old) ways of learning grammar.

You have to get into a *new* approach, a *new* way, which views grammar differently, and which helps you learn English *faster.*

When you finish the section on 'sentences', you will be introduced to three *funny* terms:

BabyVerbs
Non-BabyVerbs
HelpingVerbs

At the end of this chapter, you will put what you learned into practice by making sentences right away. Using the word '*thank*' you can:

    a. *complain about* your coworkers
    b. *play tricks on* your coworkers

A.   *What is a sentence?*

This is what this whole book is all about. If you know what a sentence is, you can *write* and *speak English* with *confidence*, and of course, you will *feel good about yourself.*

However, there are lots of ways to define a sentence. If you have read other books on grammar, they will tell you a sentence is a complete thought. But then, what is 'complete'? What does it mean?

However, there is an *easier* way to start. What is it? Before you get the answer, finish the following task.

What do you think?

Which of the following are sentences?

- *The transformation of business*
- *No firm (big enough in scope and size to satisfy) the customers*
- *Two businessmen in search of new ideas*
- *Neither Apple nor Microsoft my favorite*
- *For example, in China, self-help groups*

Ans: *None* of them is sentences!

The exercise is a trick. Why are they not sentences? They have *no verbs.*

There is a point in doing it!

The point is to show that *verb* is:

something *big*,
something *essential to* the structure of a sentence

(You can find a similar view in the book *Grammar for English Language Teachers* by Parrot.)

That is, if a sentence is a universe, **a verb is the center.** It completes the meaning and tells us what happens, or what a person does.

B. So if verbs are so big, how do we locate them?

What do you think?

Underline the verb in each sentence.

> - *The Internet grew from military research.*
> - *I have several reasons for complaining.*
> - *The CEO talked to each of the four staff members to find out their reasons for quitting.*
> - *Most people use a computer like a PC or a Macintosh.*
> - *You can go straight to a web by entering its address in the address bar.*

Ans: 1. grew, 2. have, 3. talked, 4. use, 5. (can) go

A piece of cake (very easy), right?

Yet, there are always *traps* when we try to look for them. Read the sentence below.

> The firm was moving from selling products to selling images.

In this sentence, the verbs have two parts: *was* + mov*ing*. (Past Continuous Tense)

Yet sometimes the same form (*was* + *ing)* is not a verb.

Read the sentence in trap no. 1:

B1. *Trap* No. 1

> *The business trip to the USA was tiring.*

In this sentence, 'tiring' is *not a verb*, only 'was' is. Some more obvious examples are:

1. **Building** a new business model is less than easy. ('building' is *not* a verb)

2. A CEO avoids **making** wrong decisions. ('making' is *not* a verb)

3. **Leading** a team is not about **giving** orders. ('leading' and 'giving' are not verbs)

B2. *Trap* No. 2

> **Thanks VS Thank you**

'Thanks' and 'Thank you' are common. But do some thinking. There are two questions for you:

1. Why is there a 's' at the end of 'Thank**S**.'

2. If you can say 'Many thanks', what about, '*Many thank you*'?

The answers to the two questions show that *verbs* are *really important* in English (or Business English) as one of the "thank" is a verb.

So, which 'thank' is a verb?

<u>Thanks</u> VS <u>Thank</u> *you*

The first 'thanks' is *not a verb*. It means more than one thanks, which is why there is a 's'.

B2a. Thanks *as a noun*

In other words, 'Thanks' is a *noun*. So, we have expressions such as:

Lots of *thank<u>s</u>*!
Thank<u>s</u>   in advance
Thank<u>s</u>   for your help.
(Many) *thank<u>s</u>*   for your information.

(All the thanks come with an '*s*')

B2b. Thank *as a verb*

The second 'thank' is a *verb*. But you may ask:

Who thanks *who*?

Actually it is:

I thank you.

FeelGoodTip

But you usually *skip the 'I'* when saying 'thank you'.

Other examples of using 'thank' as a verb include:

a. *Thank* you for coming to this presentation.

b. The CEO *thanked* me for giving such a good presentation.

So, since you have learnt the difference between 'thank' as a verb and 'thank' as a noun, you may ask: *So what?* It is *nothing big*, nothing really important.

Well, think again. Because you are going to learn how to make *a complaint that doesn't look like a complaint* with 'thank' (in the later section of Making Sentences).

But for now, you have to face a *bigger* question: if verbs are important, then *how many* verbs are there?

C. So if verbs are so big, how many verbs are there?

Now, you know that verbs are big. But there are *so many verbs* in English, right? What are you going to do with it?

Well, you don't have to care about the number of verbs in English. But *to make things easier* and *make you feel better*, we put them into groups (different categories).

Luckily, there are **only three** groups of verbs.

Group 1	Baby Verbs
Group 2	Non-Baby Verbs
Group 3	Helping Verbs

Baby and Non-Baby Verbs? *Am I kidding*?

Well, you'll know *what* they are.

C1. Group 1: *Baby* Verbs

What are Baby Verbs? Underline the verbs in the following sentences, and you'll get the answer.

What do you think?

1. Marketing isn't a single event or technology.
2. Many Korean gadgets are already available on the local market.
3. The global economy is gloomy.

Ans: 1. is, 2. are, 3. is

In most grammar books, these words are called *'be'*:

e.g. is/am/are/was/were/been

But in this book they have a funny name: *Baby Verbs*. Why? They *do nothing* at all. They have *no actions* whatsoever.

They are *sticky* that they link the left and the right, as indicated in the table below.

Left	+	Right

The global economy < ----------- *is* ---------------> *gloomy (bad)*

Other verbs that are sticky include:

sound	**seem**	**look**
feel	**appear**	**remain**

Why are they Baby Verbs? It is because that they are similar to *'is'*. For example, being asked by your boss what you think about a proposal, you may say:

It *sounds* good.   (It *is* good.)

It *seems* good.   (It is good.)

C2. Group 2: *Non-Baby* Verbs

If we have verbs that are like babies, we also have Non-Baby verbs. Actually, most verbs in English are Non-Baby. You'll soon know what they are. But for now, read the following sentences.

What do you think?

Can you *underline the verbs* in the following sentences?

1. The magazine conducted a survey of e-business with a review of new concepts needed to manage the new business of the e-world.
2. Organizations offering good salaries attract great people.
3. Changes to the culture of an organization require a basic change to its business processes.

Ans: 1. conducted, 2.attract, 3. require

What do the three verbs have in common? They are *not that sticky* that they don't just link the left and the right. They show that 'the magazine', 'organizations', and 'Changes' *do something* or *take some actions*. We call them Non-Baby Verbs.

C2a. How many Non-Baby Verbs are there in Business English?

There are *a lot of* Non-Baby Verbs in Business English. But once again, we can put them into groups.

There are altogether five groups of Non-Baby Verbs:

Action	e.g. run, *open*, work
H&M (Head & Mouth)	e.g. ask, *announce*, write, *discuss*, suggest
Brain	e.g. think, decide, *feel* (think), guess

Reason	e.g. cause, *permit*, require
Change	e.g. develop, *change*, become

(You'll know more about the five groups in *chapter 3*.)

C2b. How do you 'FEEl'

You may notice that there is something special about the word 'feel'. Why is it in *red*?

Well, there is something to share with you, something that is *very important* for learning grammar in English, or Business English:

that English is *troublesome*

What?

'Feel' is a typical case. The *trouble* is that some verbs can either be Baby or Non-Baby, depending on *how you use it*.

Read the following two sentences:

    a. **I *feel* good** (reading this grammar book).

    b. **I *feel* that** it's time to make a change.

You can use 'feel' of course to talk about what you feel (as in sentence a). The 'feel' is sticky that it links *the left* (I) and *the right* (good). So it is a Baby Verb.

But you can also use it at *a meeting* or when *negotiating* with your boss. That is, when you want *to get a pay rise*, you knock on your boss' door, asking if he or she can give you a minute, and then you may say what you want by using 'feel':

I really *feel* it's time (for me) to have a pay rise.

Well, can you use '*think*' instead of '*feel*'? Yes, of course. But there are some differences. 'Feel' is more personal, which sounds like you do not have an identifiable *(Explanation 3, Cambridge Online*

<u>Dictionary)</u> reason. What do I mean by *'identifiable'*? It means you somehow *feel that you are right*, but you do not have *very strong* support for your argument.

So in the case of asking for a *pay rise*, of course, you feel that you are right. (And I do think it is *always understandable* to ask for a pay rise.) But somehow you *don't have* very strong *evidence* to support you.

C3. Group 3: *Helping* Verbs

So far, you've got two groups of verbs, Baby Verbs and Non-Baby Verbs. The third group is a helper.

Helping Verbs

Sorry, she *won't* help you do your housework because she has some *special tasks*. You'll know what they are very soon.

But for now, look at the verbs underlined:

1.	Bill Gates <u>**does**</u> not run any fast food shops in the USA.
2.	What if entrepreneurs <u>**could**</u> develop a business plan that made start-up easier and faster?
3.	We <u>**should**</u> not stop technological changes in an era when technology is godlike.
4.	Disney <u>**has**</u> announced its new plan regarding a new theme park in Asia.

Helping Verbs do not take any action. They are there to help Non-Baby Verbs only. Yes, *only Non-Baby Verbs*. Well, that's *not fair*! Who help Baby Verbs as they are just babies? You'll get the answer later.

But for now, a Helping Verb helps a Non-Baby Verb to do *four* things:

Thing (1): to 'say' *no* (as in example 1)

e.g. Bill Gates <u>*does not*</u> run any fast food shops in the USA.

Thing (2): to *make questions* (as in example 2)

e.g. What <u>*can*</u> we do if we can't get the pay rise (we want)?

Thing (3): to *express your view* (as in example 3)

e.g. We <u>*should*</u> not stop technological changes in an era (when technology is godlike).

Thing (4): to *make tenses* (as in example 4)

e.g. Disney <u>*has*</u> *announced* its new plan regarding a new theme park in Asia.
(present perfect tense)

D. *Making Sentences*

So far, what is *the big thing* you have learned? Verbs are *so big and important* that they are not to be missed if you want to make sentences in Business English, spoken and written.

But for now, to make sentences, you'll get back to 'thank', 'thank' *as a verb* (not a noun).

But before this, you have to be honest in answering the following question:

Do you sometimes *get angry* with *your co-workers?*
(when they make you *mad* for doing something bad or stupid)

Instead of *yelling* at them, you can use the verb 'thank'. You can *'thank' them* for doing something bad, or, you can *play tricks on* your *coworkers* using 'thank'.

(Well, *don't do it to your boss.*
Otherwise, you have to *thank yourself* for making such a mistake.)

There are usually *three* ways to 'thank' them

D1. Using 'Thank' to *Blame* Somebody

Yes, you're right, you can use the verb 'thank' to *blame* somebody who *made a mistake.*

Sample Sentence
We can *thank Mr Trouble* for the trouble (he made).

D2. Using 'Thank' to *Stop* Others *from Interrupting* You

Do you get angry if *Mr or Ms Trouble* keeps interrupting you at a meeting? If the answer is positive, 'thank' him or her.

Sample Sentence
I'll thank you not to interrupt me **again.**

Another example:

When you are *really angry* with your coworkers and you want to tell them to *leave you alone*, you may also 'thank' them:

I'll thank you to mind your own business.

D3. Using 'Thanks' to *Complain about* Lazy Teammates

What do you think of your teammates? Are they all as *hard-working* as a *cow*? Or do some of them receive paychecks without putting many efforts in work that you have *sleeping partners* (not *sleeping beauties*)? Do they *take a nap* during office hours?

Sample Sentence
Our team did it, **but *no thanks to you.***

Key Points

- **Verbs are the *center* of sentences, as they**

  - tell you what happens
  - what a person does

- **There are *three groups* of verbs:**

  - Baby Verbs

  - Non-Baby Verbs

  - Helping Verbs

- **You can '*thank*' your coworkers for their doing something *bad*.**

(Some of the) Sentences to Make

Situation	Aim	Sample Sentence
At a meeting	To *defend* your points	This *is* for the benefit of (our company).
	To *challenge* others To *summarize* decisions	Why *is* the report important (to our company)? The decision *is* to cut cost.
Negotiating	To *make an offer*	The offer *is* firm (for 7 working days).
	To *get a lower price*	There *is* a big difference between (your prices) and (those of other competitors).
Casual Talk	To *express your opinions*	The interviewee *appeared* (disorganized) and (confused).
Talking to coworkers	To *express your anger*	*Is* that the best (you could make)?

B elieve it or not! This chapter is about *babies*. You'll see how babies can help you move your (Business) English to another level, of course, a *higher* one.

But you have to *change* something. You have to change your way of thinking about *babies*. What is it?

Babies suck.

What do I mean? 'Suck' is American slang. It means that something or somebody is *really, really* bad *(a video on 'suck')*.

So, in this chapter, you'll learn that a baby *doesn't* suck. Baby Verbs are *powerful*, so powerful that they help you to:

a. *express your anger* to your coworker

b. *defend* and *summarize* your points

c. *challenge* others

d. *make* an *offer* (when negotiating)

e. *get* a *lower price* (when negotiating)

But before you move to another level, you have to know one thing: how to tell a *Baby Verb* from a *Non-Baby Verb*.

A. *Two Types of Sentences ONLY?*

Before you get started, a piece of *good news* for you. There are only two types of sentences in English. Yes, you are right, only two.

Two only? Yes, when you focus on verbs, the center of sentences, there are only two types of sentences only.

What are they?

Sentences with *Baby* Verbs

Sentences with *Non-Baby* Verbs

So in other words, if you have a deep understanding of what the two verbs are, you can *speak* and *write* (business) English *with confidence*.

And, you can also write a *long* sentence like the following (with *confidence*):

The starting point for any good discussion is a shared understanding of the aim of a company.

Well, before you get more *confident*, before you feel better about yourself, you have to know the *differences* between Baby and Non-Baby Verbs. So, *are you ready*, baby?

Well, in the following, you will have to *make a decision*. What decision is it?

What do you think?

The decision to make is:

Are the following sentences *correct?*

1. Where *are* you from?

2. Where do you **come** from?

3. Where *are* you come from?

Ans: Only 1 & 2 are correct.

3 is *absolutely* wrong.

(Where **are** you **come** from? **Wrong!!!!**)

Why? In sentence 1, the verb is 'are', and it is a *Baby* Verb.

Where *are* you from?

However, in sentence 2, the verb is 'come' and it is a *Non-Baby* Verb ('do' is a helping verb, turning the sentence into a question).

Where do you *come* from?

Yet, you find *both* a Baby and a Non-Baby Verbs in sentence 3.

In English sentences, you *either* use a Baby Verb or a Non-Baby Verb. They usually *don't go together* in a sentence.

Where *are* you *come* from? *[WRONG]*

Baby Verb	Non-Baby Verb
are	come

So the rule, *the rule of babies*, is:

Baby Verbs VS *Non-Baby* Verbs

For easy memory, either **you are a baby** or **you are not a baby**. You can't be both, can you?

Common examples in the two groups of verbs are:

Group (1) **Baby Verbs:**

> be / *is* / am / *are* / was / *were* / being/ *been*

Group (2) **Non-Baby Verbs:**

> work / *discuss* / suggest
> / think / *decide* / guess / *develop*

With Baby and Non-Baby Verbs in mind, you will move on to a *typical* mistake.

Typical mistake: I am fully agree with you. *(WRONG)*

You may *apply* the rule to the following sentence.

Situation	At a meeting
Aim	To agree with somebody

I am fully agree with you.

The sentence is *absolutely, definitely, totally* wrong. 'Am' is a Baby Verb while 'agree' is a Non-Baby. So, when *applying the rule* that you are either baby or non-baby, you have *two* ways.

a. With a *Baby* Verb (*am*)

   ### I *am* totally with you.

b. With a *Non-Baby* Verb (*agree*)

   ### I fully *agree* with you.

So next time, when you *agree with* Mr Right, either be a Baby or a Non-Baby.

Further examples (for *agreeing*) are:

Baby Verbs	Non-Baby Verbs
That *is* (That's) not a bad idea.	I *can't agree* with you more. (Yes, it means you *agree with* Mr Right.)
I *am* (I'm) fond of the idea of building a new team.	You can *say* that again.

B. Babies or Non Babies

What do you think?

Read the following two sentences. *Which* one is a sentence with a *Baby* Verb and *which* one a *Non-Baby* Verb?

1. The starting point for any good discussion is a shared understanding of the aim of a company.
2. In 2001 Apple launched its iPod brand of portable media players.

In sentence 1, the verb is 'is', a *Baby* Verb linking the left and the right as shown below:

1. The starting point for any good discussion	is (Baby)	a shared understanding of the aim of a company

In the second sentence, the verb is 'launched', a *Non-Baby* Verb showing that a company (Apple) does something to its products (iPod).

2. (In 2001) Apple	launched (Non-Baby)	its iPod brand of portable media players

But what about the following sentence:

I *am writing* this mail regarding our order last month.

It looks like there are both baby (am) and Non-Baby Verbs in the sentence, which contradicts the rule of babies, **Baby Verbs** VS **Non-Baby Verbs.**

No, it doesn't. Taking a closer look, you will find that 'am' is not a Baby Verb, but a Helping verb, helping the verb (write) to from *a continuous tense*. In a word, 'am' (or 'be') has two identities, sometimes a Baby Verb, sometimes a Helping one.

Therefore, the verb in the sentence is a Non-Baby verb (write) in *present continuous tense*:

is/am/are	*writ(e)*	*ing*

C. *Making Sentences with Baby Verbs*

So what have you learnt so far? You have learnt that there are only two types of sentences, either with a Baby Verb or a Non-Baby one.

For now you are going to make sentences *with Baby Verbs*. As usual, it is so simple that it makes you *feel good* again. But first of all, there is a *deep* question for you.

What does a baby do *all the time?*

You may think you are not reading a book on grammar, right? But the answer to the question is really big because it helps you to *remember* sentence patterns in an easy way.

The answer is:

Nap

Babies take a nap (*a short sleep*) all the time. But here 'nap' stands for three things to be followed by a Baby Verb:

	+	**a. N**
Baby Verb	+	**b. A**
	+	**c. P**

So *what* are 'N', 'A', and 'P'?

C1. The '*N*' Way

The *first* way has something to do with the letter 'N'. So what does 'N' stand for? To answer the question, you may read the sentence:

The date of our meeting is 31 February 2XXX.

(No, there is nothing wrong with your eyes. It is the 31st of February.)

So 'N' stands for *nouns*, and there are three kinds of *things* you can talk about after a Baby Verb

1. time *2. person* *3. place*

	Baby Verb	**Noun**	
The time of his arrival	is	4:30	*Time*
He	is	our new *CEO*	**Person (position)**
The CEO	is	at the desk (In other grammar books, it is called *adverbials*, a horrible term, right?)	*Place*

However, if you think the sentences are *pieces of cakes* (too easy). You can challenge yourself by making *longer nouns* after Baby Verbs:

	Baby Verb	Longer Noun
The feature of our system	is	*the two-way flow of ideas* and *information between different divisions.*

C2. The '*A*' Way

If 'N' stands for nouns, then what does 'A' stand for? Yes, you're right again.

Adjectives

Being asked by your boss *to predict* about the future of your company, you may say:

It looks good.
(Even if you think it looks bad.)

As a Baby Verb, 'looks' here has *nothing to do with your eyes*. It is similar to 'is'.

Other examples are:

	Baby Verb	**2 Adjectives**
The interviewee	appears	disorganized and confused.
The presentation	seems	unclear and unconvincing.
The economy	remains	strong and healthy

The 'A' Way and negotiations

You can also use the 'A' way in *negotiations*.

How? Read the following case:

Situation	Negotiating *prices* with another company
Aim	To *make an offer*

When *making an offer* to a company, you may give them time to think about it. This is exactly the time you can go the 'A' way:

The offer is *firm* [for 7 working days].

The word 'firm' here is *not a noun* that it has nothing to do with a company. Instead, it is an *adjective*, meaning that something is *effective*.

C3. The 'P' Way

What does the 'P' stand for? Read the following sentences:

The item	is	_on_ sale.
The item	has been	_on_ sale _for_ three days.
The item	has been	_on_ sale _for_ three days _in_ Asia

Yes, you are right there. 'P' stands for *prepositions*. Well, you may think this is easy, but think twice after you read the following sentence.

For three days *in* Asia the item has been *on* sale.

What is special about the 'P' way is that 'P' is like your *mobile* that you can *move* it, usually to the *beginning* or to the *end* of a sentence.

Now, read the following case.

The Case of 'Out of'

A case: In *response* to *inquiries* about a product,

what are you going to write in your *email*

if you have the following *information*?

- The product is *out of stock*.
- The period is *three days*.

There are (at least) *2 ways* to do it with this team.

The first is:

- **The product has been _out of_ stock _for_ three days.**

Yet, you can *move* 'for three days':

- **_For three days_ the product has been _out of_ stock.**

Moreover, you can add '*FYI*' (For your information) to the sentence to make it sound more *polite* and *official*.

For your information,
> the product has been
>> *out of* stock
>>> *for* three days.

Teamwork of Prepositions

If you want to *push* your *Business English* to *a higher level,* you have to pay more attention to *Baby Verbs* and *Prepositions* (e.g. at, on, in).

That is, you have to think about prepositions *differently*.

Usually, prepositions come as a single word (such as of), for example:

The company is the world's leading provider <u>of</u> flexible, high quality delivery service.

In the above sentence, there is only *one* preposition.

Yet, if you think *teamwork* is better than working alone, if you want to make your presentation more '*powerful*', you have to focus on *teamwork* of prepositions.

That is, prepositions come in different forms: *one-word* prepositions or *more-than-one-word* prepositions. The more-than-one-word prepositions are members of a team: a *teamwork* of prepositions.

Read the following example:

In a *meeting* when you have to *defend your arguments,* you may say:

This is *for* the benefit *of* our company.

There is *a team* in the above argument that is formed by *two* prepositions. They are:

for .... of

Other examples include:

This is **<u>for the sake of</u>** clear presentation.
Our company will be **<u>in touch with</u>** the shipper.

Another Team: Between . . . And

This team, 'between . . . and', is very useful (if not *practical*) that they can help you *negotiate* with another company.

Situation	Negotiating prices with another company
Aim	To *get a lower price*

Does this *happen* to you or your company? You get *a quotation of* prices from another company but find *the prices too high*. What would you say in response to such a quotation?

Your prices are too high.

This may be one way of doing it. But it sounds *too direct*, and not tactful enough, right?

What about employing *the team of 'between . . . and'*?

There is a big difference *between*
 your prices
 and
 those of other competitors.

So the *advantages* of employing the team of prepositions are:

a. *Avoiding criticizing* another company (the prices being too high) directly.
b. Attempting to say (indirectly) that you *have also checked* the prices of other companies.

D. *Making Questions with Baby Verbs*

Well, I think you've got the point now.

What is it?

Baby Verbs are *more powerful* than you think. They don't just take a NAP. They help you to *express your emotions* (e.g. anger) to some of your coworkers.

But before you know how to do it, you have to take a look at *making questions* with *Baby*-Verbs.

In fact, it is *easy* to use a Baby Verb to make a question. What you have to do is to move the baby, the Baby Verb, *to the left* (of a sentence).

For example, upon introducing a new member to your team, you may say:

This *is* Mr Power.

But if you are not sure who the new person is, you make say:

Is that Mr Power?

A piece of cake, right?

Yet, you can *express your anger* (or disappointment) to your coworkers. Read the following case:

Situation	Being angry with a report written by your junior (Shirley)
Aim	To *express your anger* with a *question*

> That is the best (you could make), Shirley

In the above sentence, the verb '*is*' is a Baby Verb. So to make it into a question, you move the baby (is) to the left:

> Shirley, *is* that the best (you could make)?

Or, if Shirley is *late* one morning and says that it is because of traffic jams. You may reply with the Baby Verb 'is' again:

> Shirley, *is* that a reason for being late?

Baby Questions and Meetings

At a meeting, you may also challenge others with Baby Verbs. But this time, you do it with '*Why*'.

Situation	At a meeting
Aim	To *challenge* others

> Why *is* the report important (to our company)?

Key Points

- There are *two* types of sentences only.

  - Sentences *with Baby Verbs*
  - Sentences *with Non-Baby Verbs*

- When you make sentences with Baby Verbs, *lie down* and *take a 'nap'*.

  - n = *noun*
  - a = *adjective*
  - p = *prepositions*

- You can use Baby Verbs to:

  - *express your anger* to your coworker
  - *defend* and *summarize* your points
  - *challenge* others
  - *make* an *offer* (when negotiating)
  - *get* a *lower price* (when negotiating)

Concepts to Change

	Wrong Concept	Concept Explained
1.	I am writing to *confirm you* that . . . [WRONG]	'Confirm' is a *Lonely* Verb.
2.	Do you want some coffee? Yes, *I want*. [WRONG]	'Want' is a *Friendly* Verb.
3.	*Give five*. [WRONG]	'Give' is a *Fat Verb*.

(Some of the) Sentences to Make

Situation	Aim	Sample Sentence
Email	To *ask for* price quotations	Please *quote* us your best price (for the item mentioned)
At a meeting	To *express* your *views* To *challenge* others	I *consider* the proposal a good one. What difference does it *make*?

Things to Challenge You

	Are they *the same*?
Aim: To ask for help or actions	Do you *think* you know . . . . ? **VS** Do you *happen* to know . . . . ?

What are Non-Baby Verbs?

D o you want to write and *speak* correct English? Do you want to *impress* your coworkers or bosses? Do you want to *write emails* correctly (especially when it comes to using the verb '*confirm*')?

Then, you have to learn more about Non-Baby Verbs.

What are Non-Baby Verbs?

In a word, *Baby Verbs* have no action at all (e.g. be, is, am, are, was, were, seem). They are babies who are *sticky* linking up the left with the right. (e.g. The CEO *seems* angry.)

Yet, Non-Baby Verbs (such as '*walk*') have more to do with *actions*.

Sample Non-Baby Verbs in Business English include:

a. *run* (a company)
b. *prepare* (a proposal)

Sounds easy? Yet, there is *a problem* for you to solve.

The problem is: there are *so many* Non-Baby verbs in English and sometimes it makes you *confused*, right?

What are you going to do with the problem? How can you learn Business English *faster*? How can you speed it up so that you *save your time* (and *money* as well)?

A. *How many Non-Baby Verbs are there?*

Well, one way to do this is to put Non-Baby Verbs *into folders*, just like what you do to the files on your computer. So what are the *folders for Non-Baby Verbs*?

In a way, there are *five* folders, and for now we'll talk about the first one.

He	runs	a startup in the local area.
She	works	for Apple as a CEO.

The verbs 'runs' and 'works' indicate some kind of actions that the 'he' or 'she' does. So the name of this folder is: **ACTION**.

Other examples include:

bring, move, take, and buy

The marketing department	suggested	moving the headquarter to China.
We	have discussed	the problem twice this month.
I	am writing	to apply for the post of CEO.

What do the three verbs have in common? They are verbs about your hands and mouths, so they are H&M verbs (Well, nothing to do with any clothes shops). They are verbs of **HAND & MOUTH.**

Other examples are:

ask, announce, and discuss

I	think	there is something wrong with this proposal.
Our company	has decided	to open a new branch.

So the verbs 'think' and 'decide' imply no actions at all, and they have nothing to do with your hands and mouths. However, they have something to do with your brain. They are **BRAIN** verbs.

Other examples include:

feel (think), guess, doubt, and *study.*

Folder 4 includes verbs that have something to do with '*why*'. Why does something happen? *What* makes it happen?

So, it is the Folder of *REASON*.

Folder 4

Our new invention	facilitates	the process of quality control.
This new app	enables	the exchange of information in less than one second.

Other examples include:

cause, allow, require

Folder 5

The company	developed	a chain of fast food shops.
The world economy	began	to recover from regression.

Verbs in folder 5 are verbs of *CHANGE*. They are *on the move* all the time, like a river, and the sea, that it is hard for them to stop.

Other examples include:

increase, decrease, reduce, become

So, to sum up *the 5 folders* are:

Action	e.g. run, open, work
Head & Mouth (H&M)	e.g. ask, announce, write, discuss, suggest
Brain	e.g. think, decide, feel (think), guess

Reason	e.g. cause, permit, require
Change	e.g. develop, change, become

B. *Making Sentences with Non-Baby Verbs*

B1. A Typical *Mistake*

Sorry that we have to start with something negative. Yet, as a learner (whose *first language* is *not English*), what do you think about the situation followed?

Situation	Your business partner is (BP) offering you *a cup of coffee*

BP	Do you want a cup of coffee?
You	Yes. I want. *[WRONG]*

'I want' is *absolutely* wrong. In Asian languages (such as Chinese) there is nothing wrong with:

I + want + *nothing*

Yet, in English things are different, *really really* different. Some Non-Baby Verbs are very *friendly* that they are followed by their *friends:* someone or something.

We have a name for this kind of Non-Baby Verbs. We call it *Friendly (Non-Baby) Verb.*

B2. What are *Friendly* Verbs?

Friendly Verbs are so friendly that they are followed by friends *all the time.*

Who are their friends?

Think about the *slogans* of some international companies:

Example (*1*)   **Just Do   + *it***

Example (*2*)   **I'm loving   + *it***

You may ask yourself questions regarding the 1st example.

Just do **what?**

The '*what*' is something, right? So the Non-Baby Verb 'do' has to be followed by *something*, such as 'it'.

Similarly, in the 2nd example, you may ask yourself a question:

What are you loving?

Once again, the Non-Baby Verb 'love' is friendly that it followed by 'it'

In *business* English, other Friendly Non-Baby Verbs followed by something include:

Example (*3*)   **He admitted *the charges* (against him).**

Example (*4*)   **A customer has accepted *our special offer*.**

In the four examples, the four Non-Baby Verbs are followed by 'it, the charges, and our special offer'. They are all *things*, right?

Yet, for some Non-Baby Verbs the situations are different. They *can be followed* by *somebody*, or some guys.

Examples of verbs followed by somebody include '*advise*' and '*warn*':

The CEO advised *him* to put Plan B into action.

The director warned *him* not to put Plan B into action.

B2. *'Confirm'*: A *Lonely* Verb

So far, you have learned that some Non-Baby Verbs are *friendly* that they are either followed by:

    a.   *something* (e.g. admit + *an offer*),
                or
    b.   *somebody* (e.g. warn + *him* not to . . . .)

(It) seems *easy*, right?

Yet, read the following example from an email.

I am writing to confirm you that our company has received your delivery.

[WRONG]

Well, what's *wrong* with the sentence?

Now read it again:

I am writing to *confirm you* that our company has received your delivery.

[WRONG]

Unlike 'admit' or 'warn' 'confirm' is *not* so friendly. It has its character that it is a *Lonely* Verb.

What is a *Lonely* Verb?

It *doesn't* want to be followed by *anyone*, *anybody*, or *any guys*.

So the **FeelGoodTip** is:

Leave 'confirm' *alone!*

'Confirm' is followed by *things* only, as in the examples followed:

	confirm	*your travel arrangements*
I am writing to	confirm	*the date of our meeting*
I am writing to	confirm	*your appointment*

In a word 'confirm' is a Non-Baby Verb with 'strong character' that it is followed by *things only*.

So, now you probably know *how to correct* the sentence:

I am writing to *confirm you* that our company has received your delivery.

[WRONG]

How? Just 'cut' the person, 'you':

I am writing to *confirm*

that our company has received your delivery.

B3. The *Two Sizes* of Friendly Verbs

Well, there are *more* you have to know about Friendly Verbs.

They come in *two sizes*. Large and small?

You'll get the answer soon. But before you know which two sizes they are, you have to *give me something*. What is it that you have to give me:

FIVE

Not five *girls*, but five *fingers*. Yes, you have to **Give Me Five**.

If you watch TV or movies to learn spoken English, you must have come across *Give Me Five*, right?

However, there was a time when I heard someone say 'Give five.' Is it correct? Are there any differences between:

Give five and Give me five

In terms of *meaning*, there is *not much difference* between the two. That is, when someone says Give five or Give me five, you will do the same action, right?

So, once again, is *Give five* correct?

Absolutely . . . . *WRONG!*

Why? When you read grammar books, they will tell you the verb 'Give' takes two nouns (a person + a thing), but they do **Not** tell you *why*.

Well, bad news and good news.

The bad news is *nobody* knows why, why grammar books do not explain it. It may be due to the fact that people who speak English *as a first language* have been doing it since long time ago, and it is so *natural* that nobody cares to ask why.

The good news is: you can be *playful* about Friendly Verbs.

What is *playful*?

Treat English as *a toy*.

That is, you may *group* (Friendly) Verbs into types according to how *slim* (or *fat*) they are.

No, I am *not kidding*, you may divide them into two groups according to their *figure*, that is:

how *slim* they are
how *fat* they are

So, Friendly Verbs come in *two sizes*:

Group A:  **Slim Verbs**

Group B:  **Fat Verbs**

Slim Verbs are verbs (such as 'take' or 'like') that are followed by *one* noun only. What can you imagine? Imagine that a noun is like *a hot dog*.

And for Slim Verbs, they are followed by one hot dog (a noun) *only*, which is why they are slim.

Examples of slim verbs include:

	Verb followed by a noun (a hot dog)	Noun / Pronoun
	Take	it
I	like	it

On the contrary, 'give' is not a Slim Verb. It eats *two hot dogs* a day that it is a Fat Verb. So we have:

Fat Verb	*1st Hot Dog*	*2nd Hot Dog*
Give	*me*	*five*
Give	*me*	*a break*
Buy	*me*	*a drink*
Show	*me*	*the way*

B4. The case of *Consider*

With *Fat Verbs* in mind, you'll consider '*consider*'.

When you want to say something, or *express your views* at a meeting, you can use 'consider':

I consider   ***this proposal***   ***a good one.***

So, 'consider' is also a *Fat* Verb that it eats *two hot dogs* a day. And *the two hot dog*s are:

1. **this proposal**
2. **a good one**

C. Making Questions with Non-Baby Verbs

When making sentences with Non-Baby Verbs, you have to think about something else, something not related (directly) to grammar. *What* is it?

a movie

Am I kidding? No, I am not! And I don't think you have time for that. What I mean is you have to think about *3D* movies.

With Non-Baby Verbs you have to add 3D (*Do, Does, Did*) to make a question.

How? Read the following situation.

Situation	Discussing the *number* of customers

You *have* enough customers (to meet our orders).

Do you *have* enough customers (to meet our orders)?

For a *yes-no* question like the above, it is easy to make a question. You just pick one of the words from the *3D* list (Do, Does, Did) and put it to the beginning.

For '*wh*' *questions*, you add the 'wh' words to the beginning:

1. *When* did you leave the office yesterday?

2. *What* did your supervisor tell you?

3. *Why* do we need to reduce costs

[when the company is already earning huge profits]?

4. *When* will the meeting end?

Well, what about questions such as *'Can* I speak to Ms Listening?' The verb 'speak' is a Non-Baby one, so it seems like the 3D thing does not apply, *right*?

Don't worry! You're going to get it in *Chapter 5 (or in Book 2).* But for now, to make you feel good about yourself and to make grammar easy, the 3D thing is *a good point to start* where you begin to learn how to make sentences with Non-Baby Verbs.

For now, with 3D, you'll learn *three types of questions* to make in your *workplace*.

C1. *Usual* Questions

Do you have to *ask for help* in your work? Do you have to write emails to *ask for actions* from another company?

Case 1: If the answer is 'yes', then I have two questions for you:

How do you know *if* the other person *will help you or not?*

Do you give him / her *a chance to say no?*

With *3D* you can take *one step back*, leaving room (space) to others.

How?

You can start your question with:

Do you *think*…?

For example:

Do you *think*
you could send me the information
[before the end of this month**]?**

In other words, by starting a question with '**Do you think**', you put something on the question. What is the something?

a jacket of *politeness*

Well, case no. 1 *solved*.

Case 2: You ask somebody for help, but:

How do you know if Mr Helpful has what you want?
or
How do you know if Mr Helpful has the answer?

Again, when you are not sure you can *employ 3D*. You can use:

Do you happen to know . . . ?

For example (a question from *the woman* in the *picture*)

Do you happen to know   **where my Mr Right is?**

(Well, who knows?)

Another example (from your *workplace*):

Do you happen to know
   which bank offers a better interest rate?

Well, so far the questions are *real* questions. That is, you really want to ask for help.

Yet, there are *questions* that are *not questions*.

C2: *Questions* That Are *Not* Questions

Before you know what question they are, you have to *be honest* about yourself.

There are two questions *for you*:

Why do you learn business English?
Do you want to *stand out* at a meeting?

If you say 'yes', you have to '*take*' something.

Take what?

RISKS

RISKS

RISKS

But I promise you that you *won't get killed*.

If you want to challenge others *at a meeting*, you may use:

What + 3D

That is, when *arguing* with someone, you may ask a question:

What difference *does* it make?

C3: Saying *Not* Doesn't *Mean* Saying *No*

Do you *get angry* with your coworkers (or junior)? Do they forget big things all the time?

If your answer is 'yes', you can use 3D to *express your anger*, but with the word '*NOT*'

For example:

Didn't I tell you about it (yesterday)?

Other examples include:

Who *doesn't* know (that)?

How to use the above 'question'?

You can use it when your co-worker *tells* you a '*secret*' that *everyone* knows.

Key Points

- **You can put (Non-Baby) Verbs into *5 folders***

  - Folder 1: *Action*   (e.g. *run* a company)
  - Folder 2: *Head & Mouth*   (e.g. *discuss* a proposal)
  - Folder 3: *Brain*   (e.g. *feel* that . . .)
  - Folder 4: *Reason*   (e.g. *cause* a decrease)
  - Folder 5: *Change*   (e.g. *develop* Plan B)

- **When making sentences with (Non-Baby) Verbs, remember that:**

  - Some (Non-Baby) Verbs are *friendly,* to be followed by *someone* or *something*
    - e.g. I want *the proposal.*
  - Some (Non-Baby) Verbs are *lonely, not* to be followed by *anyone*
    - e.g. I am writing to confirm *you . . . (wrong)*
  - Some (Non-Baby) Verbs *must* eat *two hot dogs* a day
    - I consider *this proposal* (hot dog 1) *a good one* (hot dog 2).

- **Add *3D* (*do, did, does*) when making questions with (Non-Baby) Verbs**

  - *Do* you *happen* to know where my Mr Right is?
  - *Do* you *think* you could send me the information (before the end of this month)?

Preview of

Chapter 4

Mistakes to Correct

Mistake	
The CEO *suggested to build* a new team. **[WRONG]**	Probably the **BIGGEST MISTAKE** in business English.

Concepts to Change

Wrong Concept	Concept Explained
Our company *planned expanded* our company. **[WRONG]**	A sentence is a like a house. You can't have *two wives* (verbs) *in the same house* (sentence).

(Some of the) Sentences to Make

Situation	Aim	Sample Sentence
Presenting your brilliant *proposal*	To tell your *directors* the *aim* of a proposal To make the aim sound *more powerful*	I propose cutting cost on rent <u>*so as to save*</u> our company. The *one and only* aim of the proposal is <u>*to maximize*</u> profit.
At a *meeting*	To talk about a *negative* result of a project To *shorten* a long question	We finished our project <u>*only to fail*</u> in the contest. The question is <u>*when to get*</u> the money.

I s English your first language? Do your *parents* talk to you *in English* all the time? If your answers to the questions are both negative, then this chapter is *important to you*. How?

It may *change* the ways you *think about* English sentences.

Yet, don't just sit where you are. This chapter asks you to finish two tasks that are *dangerous*.

What *tasks* are they?

Well, you have to be *a superhero* or *super heroine* so you must get changed.

When you finish your tasks, Mr Hero or Ms Heroine, you will be able to:

a. *correct* the *biggest mistake* in business English
b. *think about* sentences as *a wife* in *a house*
c. *talk about* the *aims* of your proposal (with *power*)

Now, *what are you waiting for*? Have you got changed?

What do you think?

But first of all, you have to read the following sentence:

Our company **planned *to expand*** our market share.

I guess it's easy to understand *the meaning* of the sentence, but the questions are:

- *What* is 'to expand'? Is it the same as 'expand'?

to expand vs expand

- Is there *anything wrong* with:

Our company **planned expanded** our market share.

A. What's Wrong with Two Verbs Coming Together?

There is nothing wrong with two verbs coming together, *only if* you are not dealing with English. In English, the sentence 'Our company **planned expanded** our market share' is *absolutely wrong*.

Our company **planned expanded** our market share.	*[WRONG]*

But *why* is it *wrong*? *Why can't* we put two verbs together?

In English, there is *a hidden rule* that most verbs should not be followed directly by another verb. But again, *why*? Before you know the answers, you have to change your clothes. Why? Am I kidding? No, of course not. You have to *be a hero or heroine* because there are two problems, two *really big* problems for you to solve. So have you got changed?

The two *problems* are:

1. A *Crash* of *Two Cars* (Verbs)
2. A *House* with *Two Wives* (Verbs)

A1. A *Crash* of *Two Cars* (Verbs)

You may imagine that a sentence is like *a one-way street* and verbs are like *cars.* What happens if two cars from opposite directions *running into each other* at full speed?

The following diagram expresses the idea well, right?

----

planned--------------> < --------------**expanded**

STREET OF SENTENCE

If the diagram is still *not clear enough*, what about this?

So to prevent any car accidents (crash) from happening, you, the hero or heroine, have to *do something about it*. What is it? You are going to get the answers after you have read the details of the second 'accident', a tougher one:

A2. A *House* with *Two Wives* (Verbs)

This time, there are two *ladies* sitting in one house. They *chat* and *chat* and *chat* and *chat*. The more they know about each other, the *more problems* there will be. They find out that they have lots of things *in common*, like the same models of mobile phones and taste for clothes.

Yet, what they don't want to know but finally find out is: they share *the same husband.*

So what is the point? My point is:

An English *sentence* is **like a house**. It can't have *two wives* (*two verbs*) in it.

Well, Mr Hero and Ms Heroine, the two wives are now *trying to* solve the problem, by having *a fight*!

What can you do to *stop the fight*? You will do something about it, right?

You have to think *different*, not about women, but *about English*. You have to group verbs into *two types:*

Big Verbs
&
Small Verbs

B.   What are Big Verbs & Small Verbs?

Although men think that *sizes* matter, in the world of English it is different.

Big Verbs and Small Verbs have *nothing to do with* their sizes.

Big Verbs are only verbs that *come first* in a sentence, pretty much like *a first-born* child in a family. In other words, a sentence is like a family, in which a first born child is privileged (given special rights).

That is, a verb can be big or small, depending on *its position* in a sentence.

Any verb that comes first in a sentence is a big one; any verb that comes next is a small one.

So in the sentence, 'Our company **planned to expand** our market share' *'planned'* is a Big Verb and *'to expand'* is a Small Verb.

	Big Verb	Small Verb	
Our company	**planned**	**to expand**	our market share.

If you still remember the two problems, the problem of two cars running into each other and the problem of two wives in a house, Big Verbs and Small Verbs are able to solve them. You may just add *'to' before the second verb* (expand), as shown below:

to + expand ----------------------> to expand (*Small* Verb)

So to get the point of Big Verbs and Small Verbs, you may *visualize* sentences.

Whenever you read a sentence, try to *look for* the first verb (Big Verb) and then the second verb (Small Verb).

For example, the following sentence will be something different.

We plan to reduce our budget on travel allowances.

We plan to reduce our budget on travel allowances.

plan   to reduce

Well, *are we done*? Not so soon. More about Big and Small Verbs are to come.

B1. *Big* Verbs

Big Verbs usually come in *two* forms:

a. **be**
b. **non-be verbs**

a. The big verb (is) in the following sentence is a grandchild of '*be*'

	Big Verb	Small Verb	
	Be		
The aim of this report	is	to discuss	the potential of China's market

So you may imagine '*be*' is a *grandfather* or *grandmother* who has lots of grandchildren:

Be (Grandparents)

Grandchildren

Is /am / are

was / were

(will) be / (shall) be

(has) *been* / (have) *been*

b. non-be verbs

Read the following sentence? Which one is the Big Verb?

	Big Verb	Small Verb	
	Non-be Verb		
Our company	**decided**	to renew	the contract with Apple.

The Big Verb is 'decided'.

Unlike 'be', non-be verbs are usually much *more active* and *outgoing.* In English there are lots of non-be verbs. The following are those important in business English.

agree   **deny**

    suggest   *persuade*

              request   **warn**

                 inform   *notify*

                       guarantee

B2. *Small* Verbs

Before you know what Small Verbs are, you have to *ask yourself a question.* To *be frank*, Big Verbs are nothing special. They are big just because they come first in a sentence.

So the question is:

Is it *fair?*
Why does a verb coming after another *become smaller?*

Well, sometimes making sentences is like being *in a marriage*. The first woman a man marries is a *wife* (like a *Big Verb)*; the second woman has to be a *mistress* (like *a small verb*).

To make matter worse, a Small Verb doesn't have many choices. After Big Verbs they usually *come in two shapes*, either with *a head* or *a tail.*

B2a. Shape 1: *with a head (to)*

> We have decided **to renew** our contract with Apple.
> It is important **to submit** your report on time.

As you can see from the above examples, 'renew' and 'submit' become Small Verbs because they come after the two Big Verbs (*have decided* and *is*).

Moreover, they have to come with a head: TO, so that they are in a funny shape:

$$to + verb$$

B2b. Shape 2: *with a tail (ing)*

Other Small Verbs are *less lucky*. They have to come with *a tail*. What tail is it? Read the following sentences:

> The CEO suggested **cutting** the budget on advertising.
> There is no reason for **giving** up the plan now.

So the tail is:

$$verb + ing$$

In a word, the two special shapes for Small Verbs are:

Shape 1 (with a head)	**to**	+	verb

Shape 2 (with a tail)	verb	+	**ing**

However, you may ask a question, probably a *bigger* one:

How do you know *which shape* to choose?

Or some even bigger questions may pop up in your mind:

Why are certain verbs *followed by to+verb*? (i.e. agree *to finish* it)

Why are certain verbs *followed by verb+ing*? (i.e. suggest *finishing* it)

To get the answer, you have to read the following example first.

Situation	At a *meeting*
Aim	*To agree* to do something

You may say:

We have agreed to postpone the deadline.

Is there any reason *why* you have to use *to+verb* (to postpone) here? To get the answer, there are three more questions for you.

What do you *think about* 'to'?

How does 'to' *taste?*

How does 'to' *smell?*

To learn English and feel good about yourself, sometimes you have to put something *into your mouth*, *touch* that thing, and then *feel* it.

Does 'to' mean *something to be done?*
     Does 'to' taste like *something in the future?*
          Does 'to' have something to do with *things to do*?

If your answers to the above are '*Yes*', you are right. 'To' implies that there is something to be done *in the future.*

So, 'to' follows Big Verbs such as *decide, expect,* and *manage,* all of which have something to do with future.

Our teams   *decided **to finish***   **the project (within two days)**

We   *expect* (our teammates) ***to be*** **hardworking.**

Our team (usually) *manages **to meet***   **a deadline.**

In fact, I guess you have been using to+verb *in your daily lives too.*

When you buy things *at a supermarket*, do you make a list? (If you don't, make one next time)

So, what is the name of the list:

      Things ***to buy*** or things ***buying?***

I guess you've got it: **Things *to buy.***

In Business English, other examples of Big Verbs plus *to*+verbs include:

		to+verbs	
Our company	***offered***	*to fix*	the item free of charge
We	***intend***	*to deliver*	the item in a few days
Our CEO	***declined***	*to comment*	on the accident

B3. Big Verbs *followed* by *verb+ing*

Before you know which (Big) verbs are to be followed by verb+ing, I'll tell you *the biggest mistake* in Business English.

What do you think?

Read the following sentence.

The CEO *suggested to build* a new team.   [*WRONG*]

Is the sentence correct? No! *Am I crazy?* Or is it some kind of joke? No, absolutely not.

When 'suggest' is a Big Verb (the first verb in a sentence), it is to be followed by *verb+ing*. Yes, verb+ing.

*Why? Why? **Why?***

If you have read books on grammar, you will find that *they just tell you the rule*, the rule that "suggest" is followed by verb+ing, and they will give you *a horrible term* 'gerund'.

However, in George Yule's book (*Explaining English Grammar*), he has come up with an explanation. According to Yule, the *thing followed* by 'suggest' is *an event*.

What does that mean? It means it is *like a noun*.

In other words, *to build* (from the above example) is more like an action and *less like a noun*.

Yet, 'building' can *work as a noun.*

You may ask a further question:

How does 'building' work as a noun?

Read the following two sentences:

a. We *shopped* in Paris last month.

b. We did some *shopping* in Paris last month.

The word '*shopped*' is a verb but '*shopping*' is a noun. In other words, when you add 'ing' to a verb, it becomes a noun, or a noun-like event.

So besides 'suggest', **what** other **verbs (Big Verbs) are to be *followed by verb+ing?***

Before you get the answer, read the following case.

Situation	*Apologizing* for making mistakes

I *regret making* the mistake (that was careless),

but I *deny having* anything to do with money laundry.

In the sentence the two Big Verbs (*regret* and *deny*) are followed by verb+*ing*, as shown below:

regret	making (*make* + *ing*)
deny	having (*have* + *ing*)

So you've got the rule that 'regret and deny' are usually followed by verb+*ing*.

Therefore, the following sentence is *wrong*.

I regret to make the mistakes. [WRONG]

'*To make* the mistakes' sounds like *you will make the mistake,* and the mistake *is in the future.*

A mistake in the future?
Odd enough!
Right?

B3a. The case of '*deny*'

You can apply the same rule to 'deny'.

Can you *deny* something that is to be done? Probably not. The things you deny can hardly be in the future, right?

Yet, there is *another* way of thinking about

deny + hav*ing* (anything to do with money laundry)

Once again, you may get in touch with your feelings. What do you *feel* about things you deny?

Do you *like* what you deny?
or
Do you *not like* what you deny?

You've got it. Usually, for things you don't like (or hate), you take verb+*ing*. A typical example is:

I hate eating out with my boss.

↓

hate + eating out

Similarly, other Big Verbs about things you don't like followed by verb+ing include:

avoid	**delay** **postpone**	*risk*

We postponed *submitting* the report (on an analysis of our industry).

So, do you like '*submitting a report*'? What can I say if you say yes! With Big Verbs like 'postpone' you can imagine it usually goes with things you don't like.

What about *things you like*? The same rule applies. That is, with verbs (Big Verbs) about things you like, you use verb+ing. A typical example is the verb 'enjoy'?

I enjoy hav*ing* lunch with my boss.

(Well, are you telling the truth?)

↓

enjoy + hav*ing*

C. *Making Sentences*

C1. With *to+verb* (1)

By now, you have learned that in English *two verbs* usually *don't come together* in a sentence (otherwise there will be *car crashes* or *big arguments* between two wives).

With this in mind, you can make sentences (with to+verb) that are *not so simple.*

Read the following case:

Situation	Presenting your brilliant proposal
Aim	To tell the *aim* of your proposal to directors

You may say:

This proposal aims *to maximize* profit (for our company in less than one year).

I aim *to maximize* profit (for our company in less than one year).

Actually, 'to' has *two cousins*:

in order to,

and

so as to

So you can make your presentation *more powerful* by saying:

In order to
> **maximize profit,**
>> **I propose cutting cost on rent.**

Or, you may say:

I propose cutting cost on rent
> **so as to**
>> **maximize profit.**

Or if you want to make it more *dramatic*, you may say:

The *one and only* aim of the proposal is
to *maximize* profit
(for our company in less than one year).

However, if you want to *announce the result* of a project, which is *negative*, you may also use to+verb, together with the word 'only'.

Situation	At a meeting
Aim	To announce the negative result of a project

We finished our project *only to fail* in the contest.

Moreover, with to+verb, you can make a *long* question *short*:

Situation	At a *meeting*, you have a long question
Aim	To shorten a long question so that it is *easy* for your co-workers to *understand* it.
The questions	There is a problem with your proposal. When can you get the money you want?

This time, you may use to+verb with the question word 'when'.

The question is *when to get* the money.

Of course, you can use other question words:

The question is *how to get* the money.

The question is *where to get* the money.

C2. With *to+verb* (2)

To+verbs are something *useful* in Business English. You can change the meaning by changing the *tone* of a sentence.

To learn how to do it, read the case followed:

Case (*1*)

Situation	At a meeting
Aim	To show your *sincerity* (even if you are not sincere)

You may use '*to tell* the truth', or '*to be* frank':

To tell the truth, I don't agree to your proposal.

Case (2)

Situation	At your *presentation*
Aim	To begin (or end) your presentation

This one sounds easy for you, right? You may use 'to begin with', or 'to conclude', as shown in the examples below:

To begin with, I will look at the issue of cost cutting.

To conclude, this presentation ends with the big points mentioned.

Case (3)

Situation	At your *presentation*
Aim	To summarize your points

In this case, you have *more* choices.

To	*be* brief
To	*sum up* / *wrap up*
To	*make* a long story short

To be brief, the outlook of the global economy is getting better.

Key Points

- **(Usually) a sentence *can't* take *two* verbs (Big Verbs).**

- **Verbs can be grouped into: *Big Verbs* and *Small Verbs*.**

  - Big Verbs *come first* in a sentence.
  - Small Verbs *come after* a Big Verb.

- **A verb can be *big* or *small*:**

  - We *finished* our job. **(Big)**
  - We came back *to finish* our job **(Small)**

- ***Useful* sample sentences include:**

  - The CEO *suggested entering* the China market.
  - I *aim **to maximize*** profits for our company.
  - The question is ***where to find*** investors.

New Ways to Learn Grammar

	New way
Difference between *Past Simple* & *Present Perfect Simple*	*A love story* between *past* and *present*.

Concepts to Change

Wrong Concept	New Concept to learn
'Will' is the *only choice* for talking about future *[WRONG]*	There are at least *four kinds of futures*.
Past tenses are *easy*. *[WRONG]*	You can divide 'past' into *two*: a. *clear* b. *unclear*

(Some of the) Sentences to Make

Situation	Aim	Sample Sentence
Negotiating	To make an *offer* or a *bargain*	If your company *could* lower the price, we *could* consider (a joint venture).
Talking to teammates	To make *suggestions*	If I *were* you, I *would* (sign the contract).

I n the world of business, *time* is everything.

In the world of Business English, time is changing. By 'changing' I mean there are *more* past and future tenses than you thought. That is, there are at least *four* kinds of future, and two types of past. Also, when you use 'if', there are at least *two ways*.

In this chapter, you will find that there are different concepts of time. There are

a. ***four* kinds of *futures***
b. ***two* types of *past***
c. ***two* types of conditions (*if*)**

A. *Four Kinds of Futures*

Before you get to the four kinds of futures, you have to get something *out of your brain*. You have to *try your very best* to do it. Otherwise, you cannot get into *your future*, the future of your *career*. Or, your career will be 'destroyed' because you have a *limited view* of future, or future tenses. What is it you have to get out of your brain? It is a 'four-letter' word:

WILL ('*LL*)

A1. The Problem of *WILL*

Am I kidding? No, absolutely not. In (business) English, there are *more than one ways* to talk about future. Thus, you *don't* have to use *'will' all the time* for future.

There are, in fact, mainly four different ways. Which four? Read the four sentences first.

1. I *will finish* the job at 6pm.

2. Our CEO *is going to* resign when profits are down.

3. Our company *is renting* a new office.

4. The meeting *ends* at 3:00pm.

A2. *Four* Ways to Talk about *Future*

Future (1)	**will finish** ('ll finish)	will + *verb*	So-called 'Future' Tense
Future (2)	**is going to** ('s going to)	is/am/are + going to +*verb*	Present Continuous Tense
Future (3)	**is renting** ('s renting)	is/am/are + verb + ing	Present Continuous Tense
Future (4)	**ends**	*verb*	Present simple Tense

The table (on the last page) shows you that 'will' is *not the only* choice. In other words, when you want to talk about future, think about the choices of *boyfriends and girlfriends* you have.

Usually you have more than one choice, right?

So, what are the *differences* between the four ways of talking about future? Before you get the answers, you have to *make something*. What is it?

A PLAN

What does that mean? Well? Well, you have to make a plan. For what? For learning future tenses in Business English.

Future (1): *Planned* Future

In English, if you have a plan, you can talk about it with *the two present continuous tenses* followed:

| **She** | *is going to rent* | **a new office.** |

| **She** | *is renting* | **a new office.** |

Similar *examples* are:

Case		Why is it a planned future?
1	I *am meeting* my client tomorrow.	Most probably: a. You *have booked* the conference room already. b. You *have prepared* the material needed.
2	We *are running* a training program next month.	Most probably: a. You have had *all the details* of the course (e.g. outlines, contents, teaching resources) b. You *have hired* an instructor already.

Case		Why is it a planned future?
3	 A Dialogue: What time *are* you *going to* be in New York? I *am going to* visit New York next Monday.	Most probably: a. The ticket *has been booked.* b. The hotel room *has been reserved.*

But is there any *difference* between '**am meeting**' and '**am going to meet**'? Actually, they are very similar that they all refer to a future that is planned in advance.

But if you want to show that you have a *strong incentive* to do something (i.e. you want to finish something), you may use 'are + going to', for example;:

I *am going to* be a CEO (in five years).

When you use 'going to', it mean you have *a strong desire* that you have probably had a step-by-step plan, and that you are not going to stop until you are there.

So you can use it at a *presentation* or a *meeting*:

Situation (at a presentation or meeting)	To talk about *the future* of your department or company

I *am going to* lead the company to another level.

We *are going to* change the way customers interact with us.

In other words, if you use *'will'*, the so called future tense, you are *less determined* and your words are *less powerful:*

Less *powerful*	**I *will* lead the company to another level.**
More *powerful*	**I *am going to* lead the company to another level.**

In fact, in the world of business, *planned future* usually refers to the following *three*:

1. Meetings
We are discussing it at the next month's meeting.
2. Appointments
I am meeting you again next Monday.
3. Visits
Our team is visiting the New York Stock Exchange next Saturday.

Well what about 'will'? Isn't it about future? Yes, you are right. So when do you use 'will'? You use it when you make *some kind* of *predictions* (to make a *guess on the future*).

What kind of predictions?

Future (2): *Predictions*

In English, there are lots of way to make predictions, two of the ways common in Business English, are:

a. predictions *with evidence*

b. predictions *with no evidence*

Future 2a. With Evidence

Before you learn it, you have to do something you are not allowed to do at office:

What is it?

Gossiping

A Dangerous Case

While gossiping with your coworkers, you see the 'girl' you gossip about walking towards you. But the 'girl' does not just walk towards you, but *with an angry face*. So what will you say to your coworkers?

You have *two* choices:

1. She *is going to* teach us a lesson!
2. She *will* teach us a lesson.

To make a choice, you have to think about:

Do you have *any evidence*?

Are you *sure* she is going to teach you a lesson?

Look at the picture. The '*angry* face' is the key. The face may serve as evidence that you are sure that something bad *is going to* happen. So the answer is:

She *is going to* teach us a lesson!

In other words, you use 'is/a/am/are + going to' to *make a predictions* when you have *evidence*.

And by 'having evidence' we usually mean:

You *see* something that makes you *pretty sure* about what is going to happen.

What about if you have *no* evidence?

Future 2b. With No Evidence

When you make a guess about the future, which is *general*, of which you don't have any evidence, you may use:

WILL ('ll)

Examples:

In the next decade, smart phones *will* still play an important role in everyone's life.

I think our company *will* win the competition.

I'm sure you *will* enjoy your working life here.

Future (3): *Schedule*

What tense to use when you want to talk about schedules?

The answer *may surprise* you. In English, we use something simple, the *present simple tense*, to talk about **schedules** (or *timetables*).

How? Read the sample dialogue.

Sample dialogue

George: Have you got the details of the flight? What time *does* it *arrive* at London?

Michelle: It *arrives* at 11:00.

Well, but *why*? Why do we use *the present simple* to talk about schedules? You may think of a schedule as some kind of *facts*. What are facts? For example:

Business *is* about making profits.

That is, if you use the present simple to talk about facts and if you 'treat' schedules as a kind of facts, then you use the same tense for both *facts* and *schedules*.

Future (4): *Offers, Promises, Unplanned Decisions*

Future no. 4 has more to do with how you communicate and interact with others, and this is also where '*WILL*' (or the short form *'ll)* comes in.

Future 4a. Offers

You use will when you offer others your helping hand.

	Will you give me a helping hand (with the files)?
	Sure, I'll take those heavy ones.

Future 4b. Promises:

	Don't worry about your proposal! I'll support you.
Other examples	I'll send you an email. I'll see you at 9am (tomorrow).

Future 4c. Unplanned Decisions

What does 'unplanned decisions' mean. It means you make a decision *at the moment of speaking.*

What does 'at the moment of speaking' mean? It means something happens and then you have to make a decision *right away.*

For example, an *angry client* comes to your office and requests a reply from you. So, somehow, you have to say something right away; you have to give them an answer *(a decision) immediately.*

> Sample dialogue: responding to a complaint
>
> Customer: There is something *wrong* with this computer.
> Officer: I'll fix it in a week.

If you can make such *a quick decision*, with *'will'*, the future of your career will be bright. Am I right?

So you're done with the four futures, and now you will meet the *opposite* of future: past.

B.   *Two Types of Past*

Before you know which two types of past there are, I will tell you *a secret* about myself. Believe it or not! I am a *'magician'*.

What?

I know nothing about  you. But I do know *how* *your boss talks* to you. There are two types of orders from them.

(Of course your boss is not he acts like one.) a commander, but sometimes

Which *two* types of orders?

a. Finish it.

b. Finish it by 6:00pm.

Which one do you like? *None* of them.

But which one is *clear*? And which one is *unclear*? The second one (with a time) is clearer, right?

So what is my *point*? My point is the same can be applied when talking about '*past*' in English.

There are two types of past:

a. *past* that is *clear*

b. *past* that is *unclear*

B1. An *Unclear* Past

Sorry, you have to meet your boss again.

At a *meeting*, your boss may say something like this:

'**JMB,** our main competitor, ***has changed* its marketing strategy**.'
(short form: '*s changed*)

Based on your boss's words, do you know when JMB changed its strategy? Or in which *year*? Which *month*? Which *date*?

Not sure, right?

But *one thing* you are pretty sure of is that:

It is *in the past.*

This is what an *unclear* past is about. That is, somehow you know something has happened but you know nothing about the *exact year*, *month*, *week*, or *date* (not to mention 'time').

Other *examples* from your boss may include:

Our profits *have dropped* (by 20%**).** (short form: '*ve dropped*)
The government *has raised* the rates of business tax. (short form: '*s raised*)

The tense used (**have dropped, has raised**) has a long name, the *present perfect simple (PPS)*.

The tense is made up of by *two* elements:

1. **has / have** (*'s / 've*)

    +

   2. **changed / dropped / raised**

Well, one question may pop up?

Why does your boss use present perfect simple (PPS)?

An Unclear Past & the Present

To know why your boss uses PPS, you will be told a story, a *romantic* one.

It was 9:59 in the morning, and Mr *UP* (Unclear Past) was sweating. He was *late* for a meeting, *a very important meeting*, a meeting that was going to change his life. He rushed into a building, hoping that the lift doors were open for him. Yes, he was right. When he arrived at the ground floor, the lift was there, and when the doors opened, he *saw a woman*. What is her name? Ms *Now*.

It was *love* at first sight. And *'then'* they had a son. What is his name? *Present Perfect Simple*.

So what is my *point*?

Present Perfect Simple (the son) is a tense that *links up* an unclear past (Mr UP) and the *present* (Ms Now).

If you want a better picture of what I meant, read the **FeelGoodTip**:

Unclear Past (Man) + **Present** (Woman) =
Present Perfect Simple (Son)

What does this have to do with Business English? You may go back to what your boss has told you (the first sample sentence):

JMB, our main competitor, *has changed* its marketing strategy.
(short form: *'s changed*)

There is *an unclear past* in the sentence. The change has happened, right? But when?

What you know is it was something in the past, but an unclear one.

What about *the present*? You can't see it, can you?

No you can't. The present is *invisible* (you *can't see it* with your eyes).

Because when your boss says something like this, it means you *have to do something* about it, about the change of strategy. When should you do it? Most probably:

now (the present)

In other words, your boss told you about something in the past by using Present Perfect Simple. And it is *you* who has to *do something about it*. That is, an action in the unclear past *makes you do something* now (or in the future).

Put yourself in your boss's shoes, your boss wants you to do something by using PPS.

Well, I guess you will start to *hate PPS*.

B2. A *Clear* Past

What about a clear past?

Well, the romantic story is *not over* yet. The second part is not so romantic.

A few years later, Mr UP and Ms Now got a *divorce*. Mr UP was so sad that he *changed his name* to Mr CP (*Clear Past*). In order to further *'cut* him *off'* Ms Now, he moved to another country.

Not just that he married another woman. What is her name? Well her name is not important (for your learning of tenses).

What is *important* is they had a daughter. And her name (which is important for learning tenses) is *PS*.

What is 'PS' in full?

Past Simple

Again, what is my point?

The daughter (*Past Simple*) has *nothing to do with* Ms *Now*.

In other words, if PPS (present perfect simple) links up the past and the present, PS does the opposite: it has *nothing to do with* the *present*.

And the story *continues*. PS (Past Simple) got married and had grandchildren. They are:

a. *last* (year / month / week)

b. *yesterday*

c. in *20XX*

d. (year / month / week) *ago*

Sample sentences include:

I *heard* about the joint venture *last* week.

Our company *had* a hard time in *2012,* (but we have recovered from it).

He *worked* for KMB ten years *ago.*

C. *Two Types of Conditions (If)*

In your work, do you have to *negotiate* a lot? When firm A offers you a price, do you have to *counter the offer*? Or when a taxi driver negotiates fares with you, what will you say?

Well, when a taxi driver *negotiates* fares with you, you probably have to say 'no'.

But, I guess you won't say 'no' to your clients or other companies. Instead, you have to say:

If   If   If   If   If

(Of course, not *five* times.)

C1. *Negotiating* with If

Well, if you want to *negotiate well,* you have to use 'if'. If you want to *upgrade* your business *English*, you have to use 'if' too. You can, in fact, use it in two ways.

Which two ways?

Read the two sentences:

1. **If you *can* offer us** a better price,
   we *could* consider a joint venture.

2. **If you *could* offer us** a better price,
   we *could* consider a joint venture.

What are the *differences* between the two?

I think you've got it. The only difference is:

can VS *could*

So what?

It seems like 'could' is the past form of 'can', right? Well, it is, *sometimes*.

But *not* for the above two sentences. Both 'can' and 'could' here refer to something *in the future*, something that *may happen*, or something that *might happen*. In a word, the difference between the two is *not about past* and *present tenses*.

It is a question of (being) *polite.*

Most grammar books tell you that 'could' is more polite than 'can', right?

But why?

Why is 'could' *more polite?*

Why is *the past form* of 'can' *more polite* than 'can'?

You can find the answer in the following diagram:

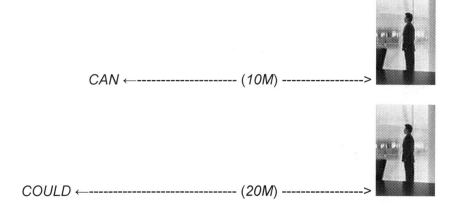

CAN ←--------------------- (*10M*) ----------------->

COULD ←------------------------------- (*20M*) ----------------->

If *can* is 10m away from a person, then *could* is 20m away. In English, the *longer* the distance, the *more polite* it is.

In other words, when you use 'could', you give the other more room (*space*), which means you are *more polite*.

So, when you want to be polite with your coworkers, you may say:

Could you **do me** a favor?

Could you **send me** a copy of the document [we discussed last night]?

C2. *Making Suggestions* with If

Similarly, you can make suggestions with '*would*' rather than '*will*', to stay yourself *away from* your suggestions, to make your suggestions more *polite*.

For example, you may tell a teammate that:

| | If I ***were*** you,

I ***would*** sign the contract.
(short form: *I'd*) |

Other sample sentences (for making suggestions) include:

I *would* (*I'd*) *advise* **you to offer more services.**

***Would* you** *reconsider* **the suggestion?**

I *would* (*I'd*) *propose* **a budget cut.**

Key Points

- There are *four* **kinds of** *futures*

  - *planned future*
  - predictions
  - *schedules*
  - offers, promises, unplanned decisions

- *Two* **types of** *past*

  - a clear past
  - un unclear past

- *Two* **types of conditions (***if***)**

  - If you *can* offer us . . . we *can* consider . . .
  - If you *could* offer us . . . we *could* consider . . .

Postscript

I have *never* thought of writing *a book on grammar*. Actually I have never thought of writing a book. However, with the digital age coming, things *have changed*.

People cannot stand listening to *long talks* any more, and what they want is *more choices*. Such is the case when it comes to *learning English grammar*. *People* pay less and less attention in class, but want more and more freedom to learn, *anywhere, anytime*.

As a tutor of English, I *didn't get used t*o the changes in the first place. I was disappointed, if not frustrated, at the fact that *teaching* started to *lose its fun* to me. Yet, 'all of a sudden', I woke up, realizing that I had *to change*, that I had *to embrace* the wind of change, and that I had *to do what I love*.

The result was this book.

Writing a book is *not easy*, especially a grammar book that is *funny enough* to make you *feel good* and learn something *practical* for your work. For me, it would have been 'easy' to write a book on grammar just explaining grammar terms clear enough. Yet, to make it funnier, I had to '*wait for*' inspirations to come, which was, I guess, the hardest part. Sometimes they came *without efforts* but more often than not, they played tricks on me, *hiding away from me*, really far *away*, beyond the reach of my 'wisdom'.

Upon finishing this book, I have learned *two things*. I know more about myself, and I know more about the world. Yet, the *two things* are *actually one*: the more you know about the world, the more you *know about yourself*.

Picture Sources

The author is *grateful* to those who allowed him to *share and remix* the following photos:

Cover Photo: http://www.flickr.com/photos/76029035@N02/6829457845/sizes/sq/in/photostream/

Chapter 1

(Pic. 1): http://www.flickr.com/photos/lululemonathletica/4312521610/sizes/q/in/photostream/

(Pic. 2): http://www.flickr.com/photos/emilylaurel/8114718545/sizes/sq/in/photostream/

(Pic. 3): http://www.flickr.com/photos/emilylaurel/8114718545/sizes/sq/in/photostream/

(Pic. 4): http://www.flickr.com/photos/mattcameasarat/6134423487/sizes/sq/in/photostream/

(Pic. 5): http://www.flickr.com/photos/27282406@N03/4134661728/in/photostream/

(Pic. 6): http://www.flickr.com/photos/makelessnoise/226654187/sizes/s/in/photostream/

(Pic. 7): http://www.flickr.com/photos/stupiddingo/8250923987/sizes/sq/in/photostream/

(Pic. 8): http://www.flickr.com/photos/ryanready/4636775541/sizes/sq/in/photostream/

(Pic. 9): http://www.flickr.com/photos/smercury98/3201467607/sizes/sq/in/photostream/

(Pic. 10): http://www.flickr.com/photos/emilylaurel/8114718545/sizes/sq/in/photostream/

Chapter 2

(Picture 1): http://www.flickr.com/photos/ideasgraficas/2570410355/sizes/q/in/photostream/

(Picture 2): http://www.flickr.com/photos/emilylaurel/8114718545/sizes/sq/in/photostream/

(Picture 3): http://www.flickr.com/photos/hygienematters/6045043367/sizes/s/in/photostream/

(Picture 4): http://www.flickr.com/photos/basykes/17582100/sizes/q/in/photostream/

(Picture 5): http://www.flickr.com/photos/basykes/2702008960/sizes/t/in/set-72157606369679627/

(Picture 6): http://www.flickr.com/photos/dylaphant07/8190436581/sizes/q/in/photostream/

Chapter 3

(Picture 1): http://www.flickr.com/photos/ryanready/4636775541/sizes/s/in/photostream/

(Picture 2): http://www.flickr.com/photos/timothymorgan/75288579/?reg=1&src=comment

(Picture 3): http://www.flickr.com/photos/gunjankarun/2641352297/sizes/sq/in/photostream/

(Picture 4): http://www.flickr.com/photos/dylaphant07/8105065030/sizes/q/in/photostream/

(Picture 5): http://www.flickr.com/photos/angel_malachite/4350119379/sizes/sq/in/photostream/

Chapter 4

(Picture 1): http://www.flickr.com/photos/jmv/2683269707/sizes/s/in/photostream/

(Picture 2): http://www.flickr.com/photos/emilylaurel/8114718545/sizes/sq/in/photostream/

(Picture 3): http://www.flickr.com/photos/f_jean/2830723220/sizes/q/in/photostream/

(Picture 4):http://www.flickr.com/photos/89619746@N02/8153022006/sizes /m/in/photostream/

(Picture 5):http://www.flickr.com/photos/ericlangleyphotography/6373055 499/sizes/s/in/photostream/

Chapter 5

(Picture 1):http://www.flickr.com/photos/alancleaver/2661425133/sizes/s/in /photostream/

(Picture 2):http://www.flickr.com/photos/fingrs/4290265087/sizes/q/in/photo stream/

(Picture 3):http://www.flickr.com/photos/en321/2589112922/sizes/s/in/photo stream/

(Picture 4):http://www.flickr.com/photos/dpstyles/4835354126/sizes/sq/in/ photostream/

(Picture5):http://www.flickr.com/photos/vokakvklim/4522913512/sizes/s/in /photostream/

References

Biber, D., et al. (1999). *Longman Grammar of Spoken and Written English*, Pearson Education Limited.

Davies, D & Pickett, D. (1990). *Preparing for English for Commerce*, Prentice Hall International (UK) Ltd.

Fogarty, M. (2008). *Grammar Girl's Quick and Dirty Tips for Better Writing*, Henry Holt & Company.

Hewings, M. (2007). *English Pronunciation in Use (Advanced)*, Cambridge University Press.

Leech, G. & Svartvik, J (1975). *A Communicative Grammar of English*, Longman.

Michael, L. (1986). *The English Verb: An Exploration of Structure and Meaning*, Language Teaching Publications.

Parrot, M. (2010). *Grammar for English Language Teachers*, Cambridge University Press.

Yule, G. (1998). *Explaining English Grammar*, Oxford University Press.

Preview of Book 2

Some of the *big* things you'll learn from *Book 2*

- ### *Complex* sentences

  - *how to* make complex sentences from simple ones
    - e.g. **How much** *our company earns* depends on **who** *the CEO is.*
  - *how to* start a sentence with '*that*' to express your views
    - e.g. **That** *our company will dominate the field* is absolutely right.
  - *how to* employ the strategy of *double ice-cream scoops* for apologizing
    - e.g. Last month I made a very serious *mistake, a mistake that* I am responsible for.

- ### Verbs in *Business Writing*

  - to correct some of the *biggest common mistakes* in business English
    - e.g. I am writing to *request for* your company the latest catalogues and prices.

- ### Verbs in *Business 'Speaking'*

  - to use the verb 'talk' to *persuade* others
  - to correct some of the *biggest common mistakes* in business English
    - e.g. The CEO *discussed about* the proposal (we handed in last week).